Life Well Lived

Luna Felis

Green Cat Books

Condolences

This book has been passed to you by a loved one who has recently passed away. Death can be a very sad time, and no-one can dictate to you how you must feel at these times. However, your loved one has carefully worked through this book to make the next few weeks as easy as possible, under the circumstances.

You will know this person, so please read through this with understanding of their character and personality.

None of the sections of this book contain legal documents, but may contain directions to find them. There may be wishes that you may not agree with or find too difficult. As this book isn't legally binding, and not intended to be, you do not have to follow the wishes. Please do take into consideration the thought that has gone into this. It has probably been as difficult to prepare as it is for you to read.

Some parts of the book may require immediate response, such as contacting loved ones, caring for pets etc. Some may be less urgent but necessary before the funeral. The last section is for you to read at leisure containing treasured memories and private messages.

<u>**Introduction for the future deceased**</u>

"Preparing for death is one of the most empowering things you can do. Thinking about death clarifies your life."
Candy Chang

There are two things that are guaranteed - birth and death. Few of us are ready for the latter, but sometimes putting things into order can put our minds at rest. Things we wish we had said to someone, but never had the time or courage. This book isn't designed for you to be maudlin and depressed, but rather to embrace life while being practical.

It is YOUR book, to record all of the important information necessary, your thoughts, comments and wishes. Use it as you will, the pages are merely a guideline to keep you on track. There are spare pages, notes sections and duplicated pages to allow for a rethink or mistake. Have different coloured pens, correction fluid, highlighters, sticky page markers, scissors and glue to hand. Tear pages out if they aren't relevant, cover the front with wallpaper (like you did at school?) if you don't like the current one. Make it your own.

Be as truthful as you can. If you think it'll hurt then put it away and just keep a note somewhere handy about where to find it when necessary. Otherwise, carry it around with you, keep it your handbag, your briefcase, glove compartment. Store it in your bedside table, give it to your loved one.

Let the decisions be yours.

*~ **Luna** ~*

<u>Contents</u>

This book has been split into "chronological" order,
according to most pressing subjects for the future reader.
However, feel free to go through it as you wish.

<u>Personal Details</u>

<u>People to contact</u>
Next of kin:

Notes about when contacting this person:

Important Contacts (eg work, clients, family, school)

Notes: (where the children are, Where you were heading ie. diary.)

I have pets that need looking after

<u>Personal Documents</u>

The following documents are stored in the following places

Will

Bank Details

Address Book

Insurance Documents

House Deeds / Rental Agreement

Birth, Marriage, Divorce Certificates

Other Documents

<u>Last Wishes</u>

This section is not a binding contract, but simply the opportunity to list some of your requests that you would like those close to you to respect. Sometimes it can be an emotional struggle to discuss matters like funeral arrangements with your family, but if you feel strongly enough about it then they need to know. Record your thoughts and wishes here, unless your family are clairvoyants of course!

<u>A Personal Message</u>
(probably worth checking the rest of the book first to check that you aren't duplicating facts ~ unless you feel you need to reiterate!)

Invitation To The Funeral Of

Location:

Transport:

Flowers:

Cremation/Burial/Other:

Type Of Service (Religious/Non-Religious):

Dress Code:

Casket:

Invitation To The Wake

Location:

Food:

Playlist:

Mood:

<u>Order Of Service</u>

Insert Picture Here

About Me

<u>Poignant stuff</u>

Whether you wish to write your own speech, choose a much loved prayer or let your family decide what to say about you, make sure that they know what you prefer.
I have given you some ideas over the next few pages, including the top 10 religious reading, non-religious poems along with more lighthearted options.
Feel free to cross out, highlight, make notes etc.

<u>Top 10 Religious Readings</u>

Twenty-Third Psalm

*"The Lord is my shepherd; I shall not want.
He maketh me to lie down in green pastures;
He leadeth me beside the still waters. He
restoreth my soul; He leadeth me in the
paths of righteousness for His name's sake.
Yea, though I walk through the valley of
the shadow of death, I will fear no evil: for
Thou art with me; thy rod and thy staff they
comfort me. Thou preparest a table before
me in the presence of mine enemies: Thou
anointest my head with oil, my cup runneth
over. Surely goodness and mercy shall follow
me all the days of my life: and I shall dwell
in the house of the Lord forever."*

Safely Home

"I am home in heaven, dear ones;
oh, so happy and so bright!
There is a perfect joy and
beauty in the everlasting light.
All the pain and grief is over,
every restless tossing passed;
I am now at peace forever,
safely home in heaven at last.
There is work still waiting for you,
so you must not idly stand,
do it now, while life remaineth–
you shall rest in God's own land.
When that work is all completed,
He will gently call you home;
oh, the rapture of that meeting
oh, the joy to see you come!"

Author Unknown

Afterglow

"I'd like the memory of me
to be a happy one,
I'd like to leave an afterglow
of smiles when life is done.
I'd like to leave an echo
whispering softly down the ways,
of happy times and laughing times
and bright and sunny days.
I'd like the tears of those who grieve,
to dry before the sun of happy memories
that I leave behind when day is done."

Helen Lowrie Marshall

Broken Chain

*"We little knew that morning that
God was going to call your name.
In life we loved you dearly,
in death we do the same.
It broke our hearts to lose you,
you did not go alone;
for part of us went with you
the day God called you home.
You left us peaceful memories,
your love is still our guide,
and though we cannot see you,
you are always by our side.
Our family chain is broken
and nothing seems the same,
but as God calls us one by one,
the chain will link again."*

Ron Tranmer

May You Always Walk In Sunshine

"May you always walk in sunshine
and God's around you flow,
for the happiness you gave us,
no one will ever know.
It broke our hearts to lose you,
but you did not go alone,
a part of us went with you,
the day God called you home.
A million times we needed you,
a million times we've cried.
If love could only have saved you,
you never would have died.
The Lord be with you and
may you rest in peace."

Author Unknown

Miss Me

*"When I come to the end of the
road and the sun has set for me,
I want no rites in a gloom-filled room.
Why cry for a soul set free!
Miss me a little, but not too long,
and not with your head bowed low.
Remember the love that we once
shared, miss me but let me go.
For this journey we all must take,
and each must go alone.
It's all part of the Master plan,
a step on the road to home.
When you are lonely
and sick of heart,
go to the friends we know
and bury your sorrows
in doing good deeds.
Miss me, but let me go."*

Author Unknown*

I'm Free

"Don't grieve for me, for now I'm free;
I took His hand when I heard Him call;
I turned my back and left it all.
If my parting has left a void;
then fill it with remembered joy.
My life's been full, I savored much;
good friends, good times,
a loved one's touch.
A friendship shared, a laugh, a kiss;
ah yes, these things, I too, will miss.
Perhaps my time seemed all too brief;
don't lengthen it now with undue grief.
Lift up your hearts and share with me;
God wanted me now, He set me free."

Author Unknown*

Life is but a stopping place

"Life is but a stopping place,
a pause in what's to be,
a resting place along the
road to sweet eternity.
We all have different journeys,
different paths along the way,
we all were meant to learn some
things, but never meant to stay.
Our destination is a place
far greater than we know,
for some, the journey's quicker,
for some the journey's slow.
And when the journey finally ends,
we'll claim a great reward,
and find an everlasting peace,
together with the Lord."

Author Unknown

If Tears Could Build A Stairway

"If tears could build a stairway
and memories were a lane,
I would walk right up to Heaven
and bring you home again.
No farewell words were spoken,
no time to say good-bye...
You were gone before I knew it,
and only God knows why.
My heart still aches in sadness
and secret tears still flow,
What it means to lose you
no one will ever know."

Author Unknown

God Looked Around His Garden

"God looked around His garden
And found an empty place.
He then looked down upon the earth
And saw your tired face.
He put His arms around you
And lifted you to rest.
God's garden must be beautiful
He always takes the best.
He saw the road was getting rough
And the hills were hard to climb,
So He closed your weary eyelids
And whispered "Peace be thine."
It broke our hearts to lose you
But you didn't go alone,
For part of us went with you
The day God called you home."

Author Unknown*

Other Religious

Death is nothing at all

"Death is nothing at all
I have only slipped away into the next room
I am I and you are you
Whatever we were to each other
That we are still
Call me by my own familiar name
Speak to me in the easy way you always used
Put no difference into your tone
Wear no forced air of solemnity or sorrow
Laugh as we always laughed
At the little jokes we always enjoyed together
Play, smile, think of me, pray for me
Let my name be ever the household word that it always was
Let it be spoken without effort
Without the ghost of a shadow in it
Life means all that it ever was
There is absolute unbroken continuity
What is death but a negligible accident?
Why should I be out of mind
Because I am out of sight?
I am waiting for you for an interval
Somewhere very near
Just around the corner
All is well.
Nothing is past; nothing is lost
One brief moment and all will be as it was before
How we shall laugh at the trouble of parting when we meet
again!"
Canon Henry Scott-Holland

You Meant So Much

"You meant so much to all of us
You were special and that's no lie
You brightened up the darkest day
And the cloudiest sky

Your smile alone warmed hearts
Your laugh was like music to hear
I would give absolutely anything
To have you well and standing here

Not a second passes
When you're not in our minds
Your love we will never forget
The hurt will ease in time

Many tears I have seen and cried
They have all poured out like rain
I know that you are happy now
And no longer in any pain"

Cassie Mitchell

Life Well Lived

"A life well lived is a precious gift,
Of hope and strength and grace,
From someone who has made our world
A brighter, better place.

It's filled with moments, sweet and sad
With smiles and sometimes tears
With friendships formed and good times shared
And laughter through the years

A life well lived is a legacy,
Of joy and pride and pleasure,
A living, lasting memory
our grateful hearts will treasure"

Author Unknown

"Death leaves a heartache no-one can heal
Love leaves a memory no-one can steal"

Taken from an Irish headstone

Dear Friends I Go

"Dear friends I go, but do not weep
I've lived my life, so full and deep
Throughout my life, I gave my best
I earned my keep, I've earned my rest
I never tried to be great or grand
I tried to be a helping hand

If I helped in a team, if I helped on my own
It was more than repaid by
good family and friends I have known
And if I went the extra mile, I did it with pleasure
it was all worthwhile

If I brightened your path, then let it be
A small contribution from my loved ones and me,
Now sadly I leave you and travel alone
Through a mystic veil to the great unknown

With such beautiful memories
That will forever be the way that I hope
You'll remember me.

Author Unknown

Do not stand at my grave and weep

"Do not stand at my grave and weep;
I am not there. I do not sleep.
I am a thousand winds that blow.
I am the diamond glints on snow.
I am the sunlight on ripened grain,
I am the gentle autumn rain.
When you awaken in the morning's hush,
I am the swift uplifting rush
Of quiet birds in circled flight.
I am the soft stars that shine at night.
Do not stand at my grave and cry;
I am not there, I did not die."
Mary Frye, American poet

<u>Or....Write your own</u>

<u>**Gravestone / Epitaph**</u>

Whether you choose to be buried or cremated, you may wish to choose the words on your gravestone or plaque. Many joke about having "I told you I was ill" written on their gravestone, but think about those who have to visit regularly. Do you want them to remember you for your humour?
Write below what you wish to have written and, if applicable, the shape and style of your gravestone.

Memories

"Don't wait until it's too late to tell someone how much you love, how much you care. Because when they're gone, no matter how loud you shout and cry, they won't hear you anymore"

This section of the book is all about your happy memories, while you are alive. Remember the good times, record events straight after they have happened while they are still fresh. A wedding, a birth, a trip to the seaside. Hopefully your book will be handy so that you can grab it to write something down.
DON'T use it to record bad memories. No matter how hurt you may feel, its not something that a loved one will want to be reminded of after you are gone.
Stick pictures in as reminders, or keep a note of where to find the photos.

Your Comments about this section

<u>Memories</u>

Do you remember....?

Date:

Event:

Memories:

Insert photos, newspaper clippings, children's drawings etc

<u>Memories</u>

Do you remember....?

Date:

Event:

Memories:

Insert photos, newspaper clippings, children's drawings etc

<u>Memories</u>

Do you remember....?

Date:

Event:

Memories:

**Insert photos, newspaper clippings, children's
drawings etc**

<u>Memories</u>

Do you remember....?

Date:

Event:

Memories:

Insert photos, newspaper clippings, children's drawings etc

<u>Memories</u>

Do you remember....?

Date:

Event:

Memories:

Insert photos, newspaper clippings, children's drawings etc

<u>Memories</u>

Do you remember....?

Date:

Event:

Memories:

Insert photos, newspaper clippings, children's drawings etc

<u>Memories</u>

Do you remember....?

Date:

Event:

Memories:

Insert photos, newspaper clippings, children's drawings etc

<u>Memories</u>

Do you remember....?

Date:

Event:

Memories:

Insert photos, newspaper clippings, children's
drawings etc

<u>Memories</u>

Do you remember....?

Date:

Event:

Memories:

Insert photos, newspaper clippings, children's drawings etc

<u>Memories</u>

Do you remember....?

Date:

Event:

Memories:

Insert photos, newspaper clippings, children's drawings etc

<u>Memories</u>

Do you remember....?

Date:

Event:

Memories:

Insert photos, newspaper clippings, children's drawings etc

<u>**Sources and Thank Yous**</u>

Top 10 Religious prayers - www.memorialprayercards.com

Non-religious poems - www.pinterest.com

*Author unknown – credits have been found for several authors

ARE YOU A WRITER?

We are looking for writers to send in their manuscripts.

If you would like to submit your work, please send to

books@green-cat.co

Green Cat Books